A World of Inventions

Cameron Macintosh

Contents

Amazing Inventions

Throughout history, people have used their brains and their imaginations to make amazing new things. These are called inventions. People have invented things for work, travel, **communication** – and even just for fun!

Many things we use today were invented a long time ago. Other things were invented more recently. Let's take a look at some of the world's most amazing inventions …

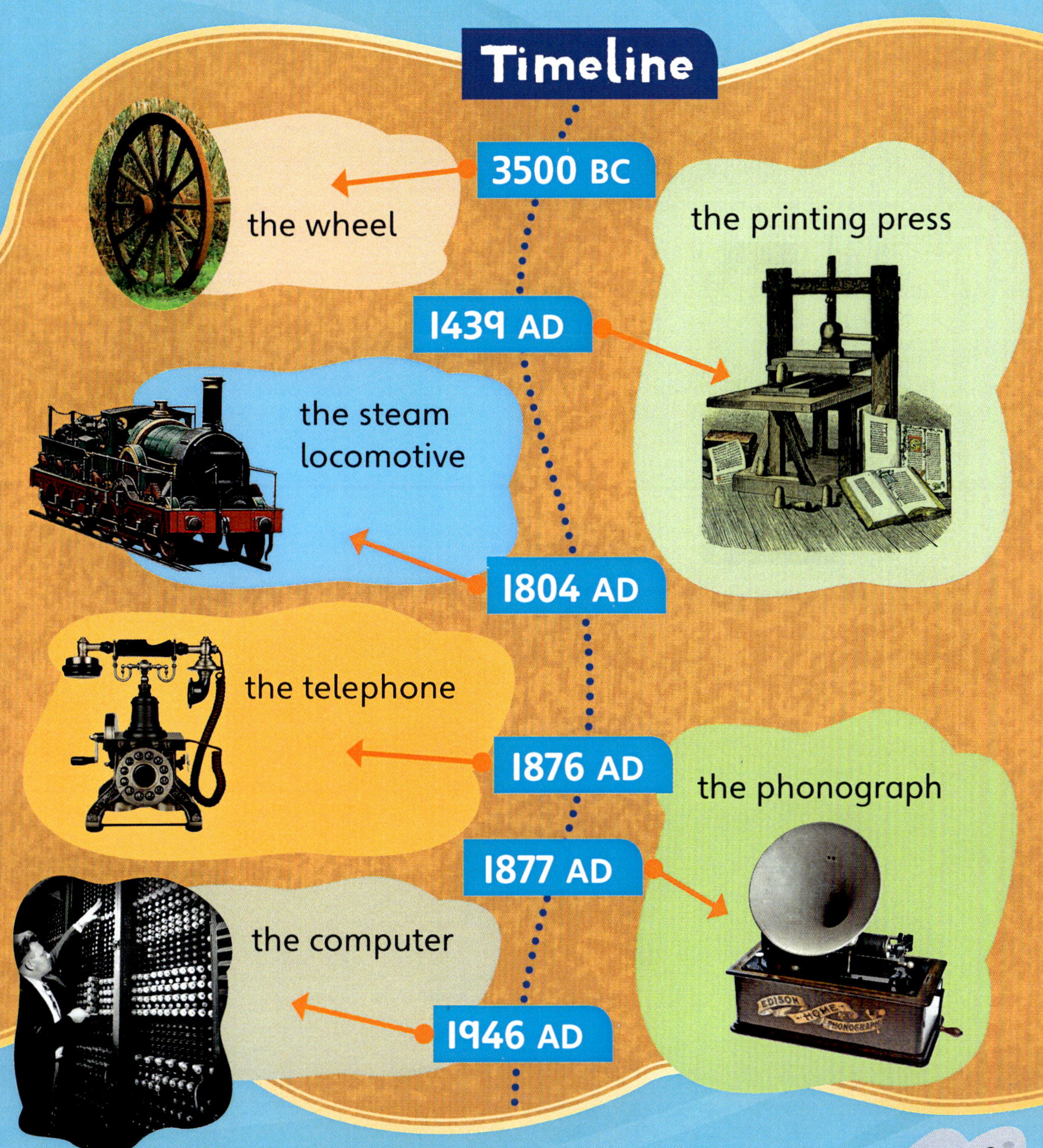

The Wheel

One of the world's most important inventions is the wheel. It was invented around 3500 BC.

Early wheels were not used in **vehicles** like they are today. They were made of stone or wood. One type of early wheel was used to make **pottery**. It lay on its side and was spun to make bowls, pots and other things from clay.

This man is making pottery using an early wheel.

This picture shows how large objects can be moved using logs that roll.

Another type of of early wheel was the log. Logs were used as **rollers** to move large objects. The object was placed on the logs and could be pulled along on top of them.

Another important invention used with the wheel was the axle. An axle is the beam that joins two wheels so they can work together. The axle made it possible for many different vehicles to be invented.

The axle joins two wheels so they can move together.

This stone model of a chariot, from around 2000 BC, shows the use of wheels and axles.

Soon, wheels and axles were used to invent carts and **chariots**. Today, wheels and axles are still used in cars, trucks and other vehicles.

The Printing Press

In the past, books were difficult to make. The words in the book had to be written onto each page by hand. This took a long, long time! Luckily, this changed with the invention of the printing press.

This book was written by hand in the year 1092.

The stamps were arranged in frames.

An early printing machine was invented in China around 1040. It used a different stamp for each Chinese word. The stamps were **arranged** into sentences and coated with ink. Then, they were pressed onto paper or other material.

In Europe around 1439, another kind of printing machine began to be used. It was called a printing press. To make a print, metal letters were arranged into words and sentences. Then, the letters were coated with ink and pressed onto paper.

Finally, people could make as many copies of books as they wanted!

This is the first European printing press, the Gutenberg printing press. It was named after its inventor, Johann Gutenberg.

The Gutenberg Bible

The first book printed in Europe was the Bible. It was printed in Germany by Johann Gutenberg.

The Steam Locomotive

In the past, travelling long distances over land was difficult and slow. For most people, the fastest way to get somewhere was by horse and cart.

This picture, from around 1820, shows a family travelling by horse and cart.

Trevithick's steam-powered vehicle, 1801

In England in 1801, a man called Richard Trevithick invented a vehicle that ran on steam. It burned **coal** to make steam, which then moved the wheels. In 1804, Trevithick turned his invention into another steam-powered vehicle – the steam locomotive.

Special tracks were built for the steam locomotives to travel on. As locomotive got bigger and faster, they were able to carry more passengers and goods.

Now people could easily travel long distances for work or school, or to visit friends and family.

This picture shows two steam-powered locomotives in England in the 1820s.

The First Train Track

The first track that was made for locomotives was built in England in 1825. Until then, locomotives travelled on tracks that had been made for horses and carts.

The Telephone

Telephones help us talk to people both near and far. In the past, it was difficult to get in contact with people who lived far away. People had to write letters, or send messages called telegrams. Telegrams were sent along **telegraph** lines using a code called **Morse code**.

This woman is using Morse code to send a telegram.

Not everyone could use Morse code. People needed lessons to use it properly. After the 1870s, communication became easier. Scientists invented ways to send voices along electrical wires. The telephone was born!

Alexander Graham Bell was one of the scientists who invented the telephone. He made the world's first telephone call in 1876. He called his assistant, who was in the next room!

Telephone lines were built around the world and people began buying telephones to use. They loved talking to friends and family using this exciting new invention.

Alexander Graham Bell

Today, we use telephones in many different ways. We can talk, take photos and even listen to music on our telephones. Bell would be amazed!

The First Phone Call!

The first words heard using a telephone were spoken by Bell to his assistant, Thomas Watson. "Mr Watson," said Bell, "come here – I want to see you."

The Phonograph

Recorded music is a big part of many people's lives. We can thank the American inventor Thomas Edison for this! In 1877, Edison invented the phonograph. The phonograph was an early type of record player. It recorded sounds and played them on a metal **cylinder**.

Edison and his phonograph, 1878

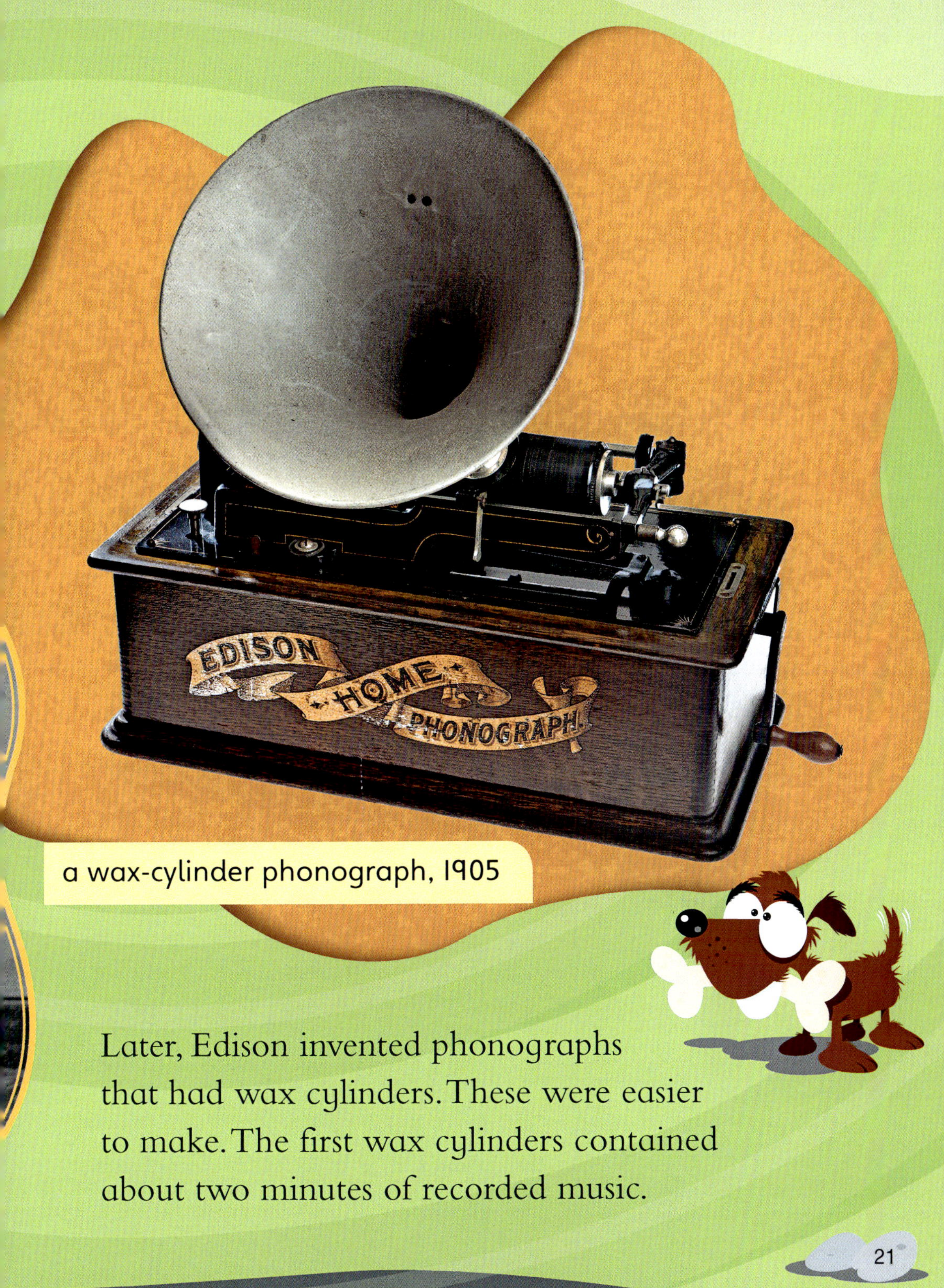

a wax-cylinder phonograph, 1905

Later, Edison invented phonographs that had wax cylinders. These were easier to make. The first wax cylinders contained about two minutes of recorded music.

Soon, another way to play recorded music was invented – the record player. The **vinyl record** spins on the record player. The sounds are heard through a needle that touches the record as it spins. Record players are still used today.

an early record player

Edison would be very impressed with how recorded music is heard today. Small music players can now hold thousands of songs!

The Computer

The world's first computers were very different to the computers we use today. They were huge machines invented to solve mathematical problems.

The first computers were a lot larger than the computers we use today.

In 1946, the first **programmable** computer was used. It took three years to build, and was 45 metres wide!

This computer was called the ENIAC computer.

For a long time, computers were used mostly by people at work. Not many people used them at home or at school.

The Apple II computer

In 1977, computer use became more popular with the arrival of the Apple II computer. The Apple II used **audio cassettes** to store information. It also had a colour screen!

Junior Inventors

Have you had any interesting ideas lately? Maybe you could be the world's next big inventor! A lot of amazing things have been invented by young people. Here are a few of them!

In 1824, Louis Braille invented the Braille reading system. He was 15 years old. People who can't see can use Braille to read. Letters are written as raised dots. They are read by touching them with the fingertips.

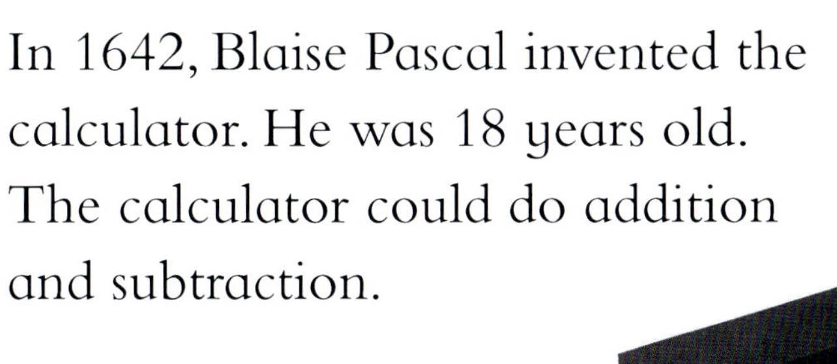

In 1642, Blaise Pascal invented the calculator. He was 18 years old. The calculator could do addition and subtraction.

In 1873, Chester Greenwood invented earmuffs. He was 15 years old. We can thank Chester for keeping our ears warm on cold days!

In 1905, Frank Epperson invented the popsicle (icy pole). He was 11 years old. His invention keeps millions of people cool on hot days!

In 1930, George Nissen invented the trampoline. He was 16 years old. He used scraps of metal and some canvas to make the trampoline in his parents' garage.

In 1963, Tom Sims invented the snowboard. He was 13 years old. He made his snowboard with a piece of **plywood**.

Glossary

arranged	put in order
audio cassettes	small cases that hold tape to store information
chariots	horse-drawn vehicles with two wheels
coal	a black or dark brown rock found underground
communication	the passing on of information
cylinder	a tube
Morse code	a code that uses long or short sounds to stand for letters in the alphabet
plywood	a type of thin wooden board
pottery	pots, bowls and other things made of baked clay. Porcelain is a type of pottery.
programmable	able to be given instructions
rollers	tubes or other round objects that things can be rolled over
telegraph	a system of sending messages along a wire
vehicles	things that are used to transport people or goods
vinyl record	a flat disc with grooves that holds recorded music.